Austin
CITY LIMIT

Super Smart CITY Series: Awesome Austin!
ISBN: 978-1-941775-12-7
April Chloe Terrazas, BS University of Texas at Austin.
Copyright © 2015 Crazy Brainz, LLC

Visit us on the web! www.Crazy-Brainz.com

Cover design, illustrations and text by: April Chloe Terrazas

Austin is the capital of Texas!

Austin was established in 1839 and it was named after its founder, Stephen F. Austin.

Austin is known as the "live music capital of the world." Any given day of the year you are likely to find someone playing live music somewhere in Austin.

Austin is full of fun things do, places to go and delicious food to eat!

Enjoy your time in Austin, Texas!

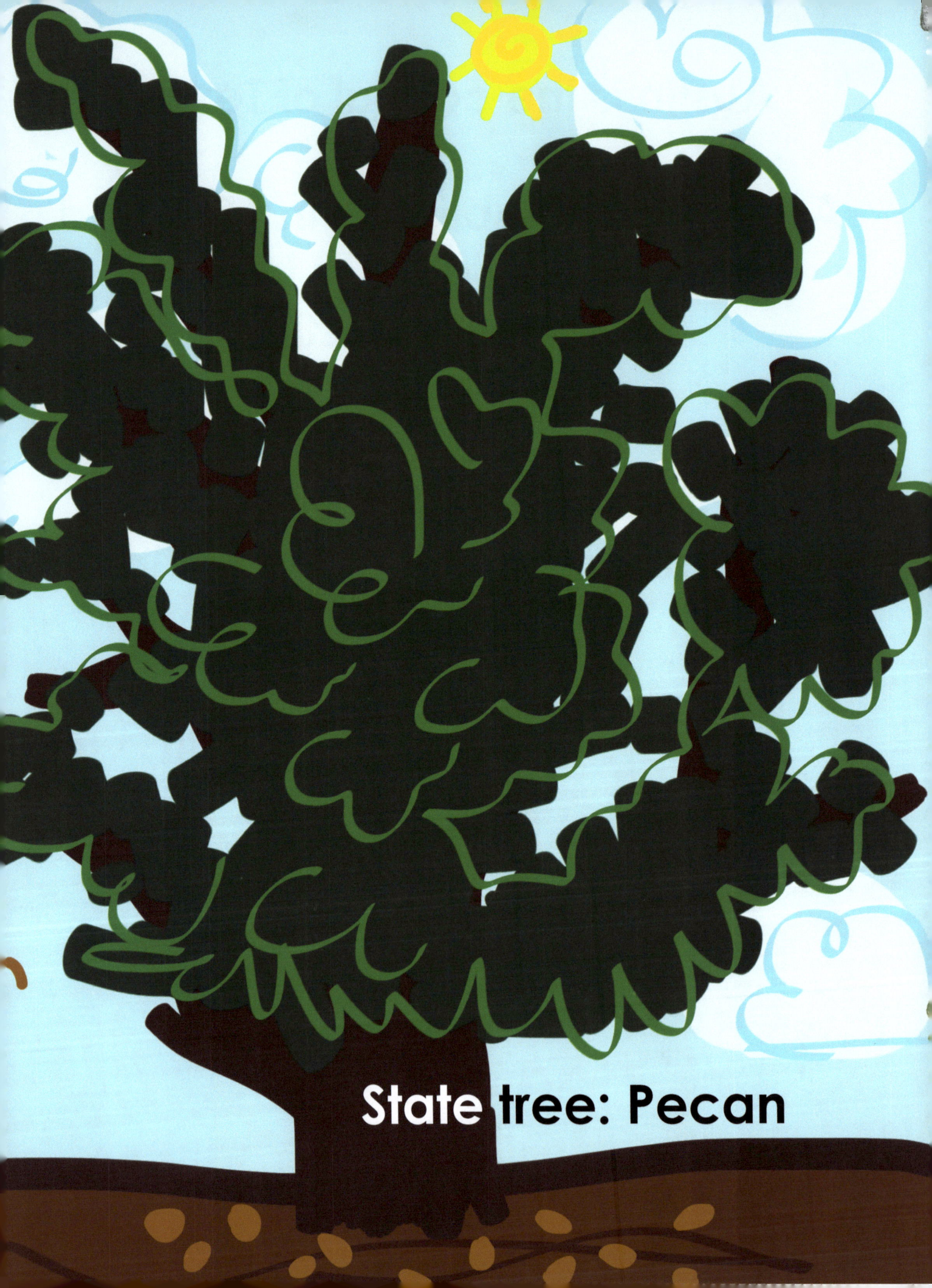

State tree: Pecan

State bird: Mockingbird

Mockingbirds like to cause trouble! You can see and hear them pecking and squacking at dogs and squirrels.

State flower: Bluebonnet

Bluebonnets cover Austin during the months March and April.

While you're in Austin, you will likely see people wearing **cowboy boots.**

When you wear **cowboy boots,** be sure to speak like the locals and say "Howdy, y'all!"

All around Austin you will see plenty of burnt orange.

This color represents the University of Texas and its mascot, THE LONGHORN!

If you drive toward the countryside, you may see a longhorn enjoying some fresh grass in a field.

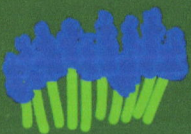

Stop by the University Coop on Guadalupe and get yourself something burnt orange!

Downtown Austin has a lot to offer a visitor. You can rent a stand up paddle board or kayak and enjoy some time on Lady Bird Lake, you can eat at many delicious restaurants and stay at one of Austin's many beautiful and luxurious hotels.

i love you
so much

"i love you so much" is painted on the side of Joe's Coffee located on Congress Avenue in the SOCO district.

There are many shops and restaurants located nearby.

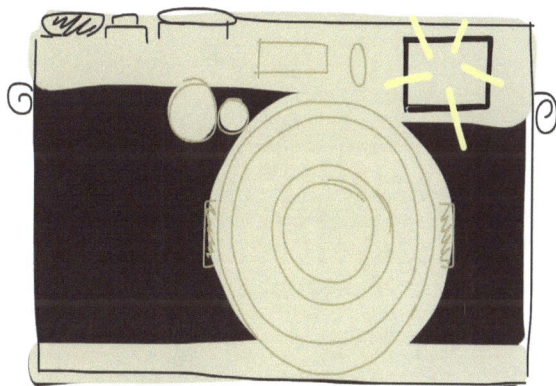

Take your family for a visit to Joe's and snap a shot.

You may have to wait in line, this spot is very popular!

Every evening at dusk, you will see many people start to gather on the Congress Avenue bridge.

There are around 1.5 million Mexican Free-Tailed Bats living under the bridge!

Every evening, they all come flying out for dinner. They appear in giant clouds because there are so many.

August is the best time for bat viewing.

Each night, the bats fly miles
around Austin and feed on
TONS of bugs!

In the winter, the bats leave
Austin and go to Mexico.
They return to Austin in March.

Austin LOVES football!

During the fall season, you will see the stadium just off highway IH-35 filled with **burnt orange**.

Zilker Park is
located on Barton Springs
Road near downtown Austin.

There are countless fields for soccer,
playgrounds for running around,
Barton Springs Pool for swimming and
the Zilker Zephyr train!

The train goes all around the beautiful
park for a 25 minute ride.
Children $2.00, Adults $3.00

The Zilker Kite Festival occurs every year in the spring. The event is free and everyone is welcome!

You may bring your own kite or purchase one there.

All of Austin's best restaurants have trailers there with delicious food, drinks and desserts!

There is also face painting, balloons, and other merchandise available.

Let's hope for a windy day this year!

In spring and summer, beautiful varieties of colorful wildflowers cover roadways and fields all around Austin.

Visit the Wildflower Center in South Austin and learn about the amazing variety of plants local to the Austin area.

Pennybacker bridge is in west Austin and is part of Highway 360. The bridge is about 15 to 20 minutes from downtown.

It is named after the architect, Percy Pennybacker, who designed the suspension bridge that does not touch the water!

There is a small, 3 acre park
and boat ramp for Lake Austin access.

Be sure to bring your camera
and/or swimsuit!

The Texas State Capitol is located in downtown Austin.

The Texas State Capitol building is the LARGEST state capitol building in the United States!

Go for a walk and have a picnic
under a huge pecan tree.

You are sure to see squirrels
happily running through
the trees and on the lawn!

Austin is famous for having numerous outdoor activities!

Be sure to have a swimsuit and towel available at all times!

Swim at Barton Springs Pool and Deep Eddy Pool in the downtown area.

Play soccer or sand volleyball at Zilker Park.

During summer, enjoy free live concerts in the park, *Blues on the Green,* and free outdoor shows at Zilker Hillside Theater.

Take a stroll through the beautiful Zilker Botanical Gardens. *(Bring your camera!)*

Walk, jog, run or ride a bike along the Hike & Bike Trail.

Rent a canoe, kayak or stand up paddle board and enjoy the amazing views of downtown Austin from Lady Bird Lake.

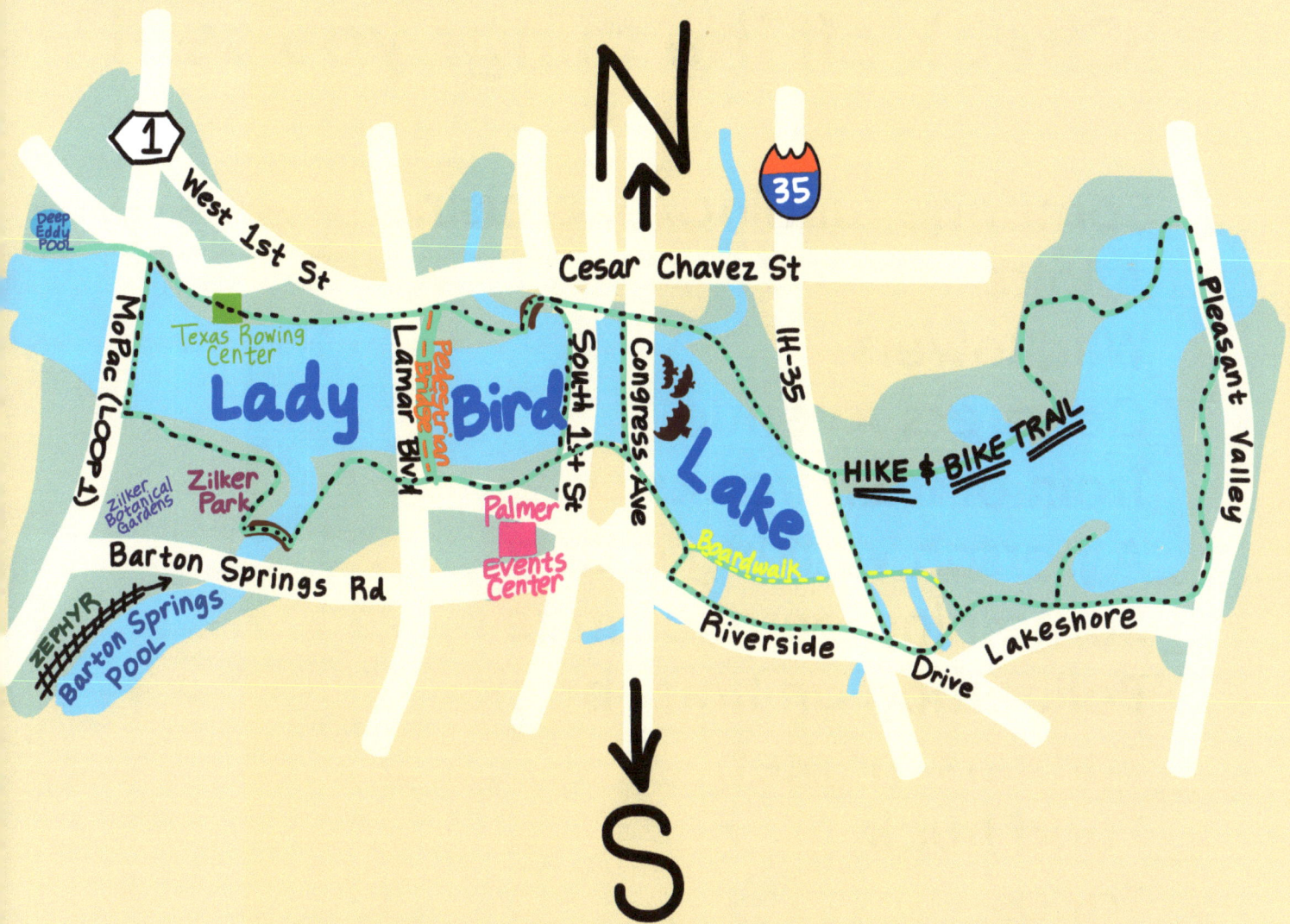

The Hike & Bike Trail has two safety features:

A pedestrian bridge at Lamar Blvd and a Boardwalk parallel to Riverside Drive.

Check off the things you see!

__Someone running/exercising
__A lake
__WIldflowers
__Congress Avenue
__Train or train tracks
__A person walking a dog
__Something burnt orange
__Policeman on horseback
__Farmers market
__Food truck
__Tacos
__Toy store
__Austin Pets Alive!
__The Domain
__Horse and buggie
__A pedicab
__A museum
__Zilker Park
__Peter Pan Putt Putt
__Kayaks
__A cow or goat
__Keep Austin Weird T-shirt

My favorite shop: _____

My favorite restaurant:_____

My favorite souvenir: _____

Where I stayed: _____

Who I went with:_____

The weather was:
Cold   Cool   Warm   HOT

Draw what the weather was like:

CULTURE:

Cathedral of Junk	512-299-7413, private residence
Casa Neverlandia	512-442-7613, facebook
Umlauf Sculpture Garden	UmlaufSculpture.org
Austin Public Library	Summer Prgm 5-12 yr olds
Austin Symphony's Children's Day Art Park	
	Summer Program	AustinSymphony.org
Pioneer Farms	PioneerFarms.org
Double Decker Tour Bus	DoubleDeckerAustin.com
Baylor Street Art Wall	12th and Baylor off Lamar Blvd
Austin Duck Adventures	AustinDucks.com
Nature Nights at Lady Bird Johnson Wildflower Center	
	Wildflower.org
Zilker Hillside Theater	
	(July-August, across from Barton Springs)

ACTIVE RENTALS:

Zilker Park Boat Rentals	ZilkerBoats.com
Rowing Dock	RowingDock.com
Austin Rowing Club	AustinRowing.org
Texas Rowing Center	TexasRowingCenter.com
Barton Springs Bike Rentals	BartonSpringsBikeRental.com
Rocket Electrics (Bikes)	RocketElectrics.com
Austin Water Bikes	AustinWaterBikes.com
Float On (Lake Austin)	RentalBoatAustin.com

PAINT POTTERY:

Café Monet	CafeMonet.org
Color Me Mine!	BeeCave.ColorMeMine.com
Ceramics Bayou	CeramicsBayou.com

ACTIVE:

Ice Skating:
      Chaparral Ice   ChaparralIce.com
      Whole Foods downtown (Dec, Jan only)
Roller Skating:
      Playland Skate Center   PlaylandSkateCenter.net
Safari Champ   SafariChamp.com

AMUSEMENT:

The Thinkery	ThinkeryAustin.org
Jumpoline	JumpolinePark.com
Jumpstreet	GotJump.com/cedar-park
Pinballz Arcade	PinballzArcade.com
Kiddie Acres Amusement Park	www.KiddieAcres.com
Peter Pan Mini Golf	PeterPanMiniGolf.com
Blazer Tag	BlazerTag.com
Glow in the Dark Bowling at the Texas Union (UT Campus)	
	512-475-6670
Austin Rock Gym	AustinRockGym.com
Alamo Drafthouse, Regal Entertainment Group	
	(FREE MOVIES mid-week in Summer)

MUSEUMS:

Austin Nature and Science Center	512-974-3888
Museum of Natural and Artificial Ephemerata	MNAE.org
Texas Memorial Museum	UTexas.edu/TMM
Bullock Texas State History Museum	TheStoryOfTexas.com
LBJ Library Museum	LbjLibrary.org
Blanton Museum of Art FREE THURSDAYS	
	BlantonMuseum.org

LIVE MUSIC:

Do512.com, Austin360.com, FreeFunInAustin.com
365ThingsAustin.com

Austin City Limits Music Festival (Fall)	ACLFestival.com
South By Southwest Music and Film Festival	SXSW.com
Concerts in the Park at the Long Center	AustinSymphony.org
KVET Texas Music Series:	981KVET.com
Wednesday night concerts at the Nutty Brown Café	

DISC GOLF:

Zilker Park (downtown, Barton Springs Rd/MoPac)
Circle C Ranch Metropolitan Park (south, 512-974-6700)
Mary Moore Searight Metropolitan Park (next to Circle C)

FARMERS MARKETS/FRESH FOOD:

Farmers Markets (4th and Guadalupe, Sat 9am-1pm)

Boggy Creek Farm	BoggyCreekFarm.com
Springdale Farm	SpringdaleFarmAustin.com

OUTDOOR/SCENERY:

Mount Bonnell (highest point in Austin at 775 ft	512-974-6700
Austin Steam Train	AustinSteamTrain.org
Longhorn Cavern (Marble Falls)	830-598-2283
Mayfield Park	MayfieldPark.org
Enchanted Rock (Fredricksburg)	

SWIMMING/WATER:

Lake Austin, Lake Travis	
Hamilton Pool Reserve (Dripping Springs)	512-264-2740
Krause Springs (Spicewood)	KrauseSprings.net
Barton Creek Greenbelt	512-477-1566
Deep Eddy Pool	DeepEddy.org/pool
Barton Springs Pool	512-476-9044
Butler Park	1000 Barton Springs Rd
Brushy Creek Lake Park	2901 Brushy Creek Road, Cedar Park
Westlake Beach on Lake Austin	WestlakeBeach.com
Emma Long Park	1706 City Park Road

SHOPPING (stores with highest ratings):

The Natural Baby Company	SoCo	512-761-2892
Monkey See Monkey Do	SoCo	512-443-4999
Bright Beginnings	Anderson	512-453-0433
Perriberri	Bee Caves	512-478-3785
Picket Fences	Bryker Woods	512-458-2565
Over The Rainbow	Exposition	512-477-2954
Wee	Downtown	512-236-1338
Toy Joy	Downtown	512-320-0090
Book People	Downtown	512-472-5050
Millie & Mox	Lakeway	512-377-1142
Sweet Love & Sugar Britches	Round Rock	512-255-6602
Sandy's Shoes	Anderson Ln	512-452-8697
Anna's Toy Depot	South Lamar	512-447-8697
Brilliant Sky Toys & Books	Westlake	512-347-8697

RESALE SHOPS:

SparkleKids	Burnet Rd	512-420-9413
Swank Baby Boutique	W Hwy 290	866-497-0004

Family Friendly Restaurants

Freddie's Place - Playscape, live music on Thursday, Friday, Saturday
   1703 South 1st Street 78704 (512-445-9197)

Smoke 'N Hops - Patio, great view, BBQ.
   3799 US 290, Dripping Springs 78620 (512-655-3069)

Boat House Grill - playscape with tables all around, umbrellas, shade.
   (Lake Travis area) - 6812 RR 620 North 78730 (512-249-5200)

Doc's Motorworks (SOCO) 1123 South Congress Ave 78704 (512-448-9181)
   & **Doc's Backyard** (South Central) 5207 Brodie Ln #100 78745 (512-892-5200)

Nutty Brown Cafe - kid's night every month (check online schedule for dates) Sandpit, patio covered by oaks. West Hwy 290 (512-301-4648)

Central Market North - playscape, live music, duck pond, delicious food.
   4001 North Lamar Blvd 78756 (512-206-1000)

Austin's Pizza (Westlake) - pizza + playscape! Play area surrounded by fence.
   3638 Bee Caves Road 78746 (512-795-8888)

Waterloo Ice House - playscape, sandpit, yummy food! (4 Austin locations)
   WaterlooIceHouse.com

Hula Hut (downtown) - Austin favorite, located on Lake Austin.
   3825 Lake Austin Blvd 78703 (512-476-4852)

Shady Grove (downtown) - lots of outdoor seating under huge trees.
   1624 Barton Springs Road 78704 (512-474-9991)

Whole Foods DOMAIN (North Austin) - playscape, healthy + delicious food.
   11920 Domain Drive 78758 (512-831-3981)

Phil's Ice House + Amy's Ice Creams - playgrounds, outdoor space. PhilsIceHouse.com
5620 Burnet Rd, 13265 US Hwy 183N, 2901 S. Lamar (512-707-8704)

The Salt Lick BBQ (Driftwood, Round Rock) - Round Rock location has fenced in playscape for kids + outdoor seating at picnic tables.
   D: 18300 FM 1826 78619 (512-858-4959) /// RR: 3350 East Palm Valley Blvd 78665

Mandola's Italian Market - outdoor eating area with playscape
   4301 West William Cannon Bldg E-1 (512-524-2222) MandolasMarket.com

Jester King Brewery + Stanley's Farmhouse Pizza - Open Fri, Sat Sun.
   Countryside, playscape, picnic tables, plenty of space.
   Southwest Austin, 20-30 min from downtown Austin StanleysFarmhousePizza.com

Draw your favorite places/things in Austin!

www.ingramcontent.com/pod-product-compliance
Lightning Source LLC
Chambersburg PA
CBHW040021050426

42452CB00002B/76